This book belongs to:

● ●

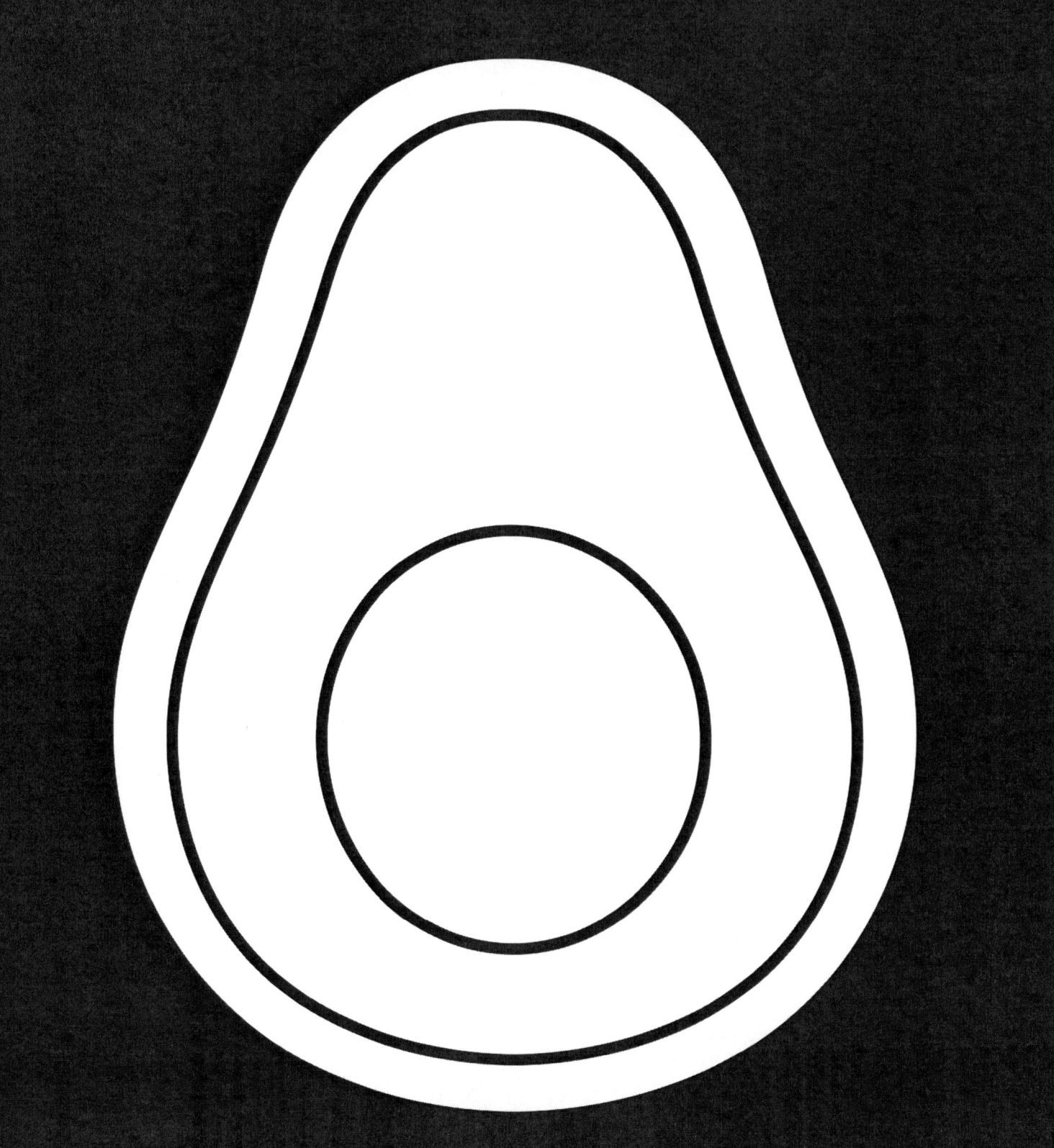

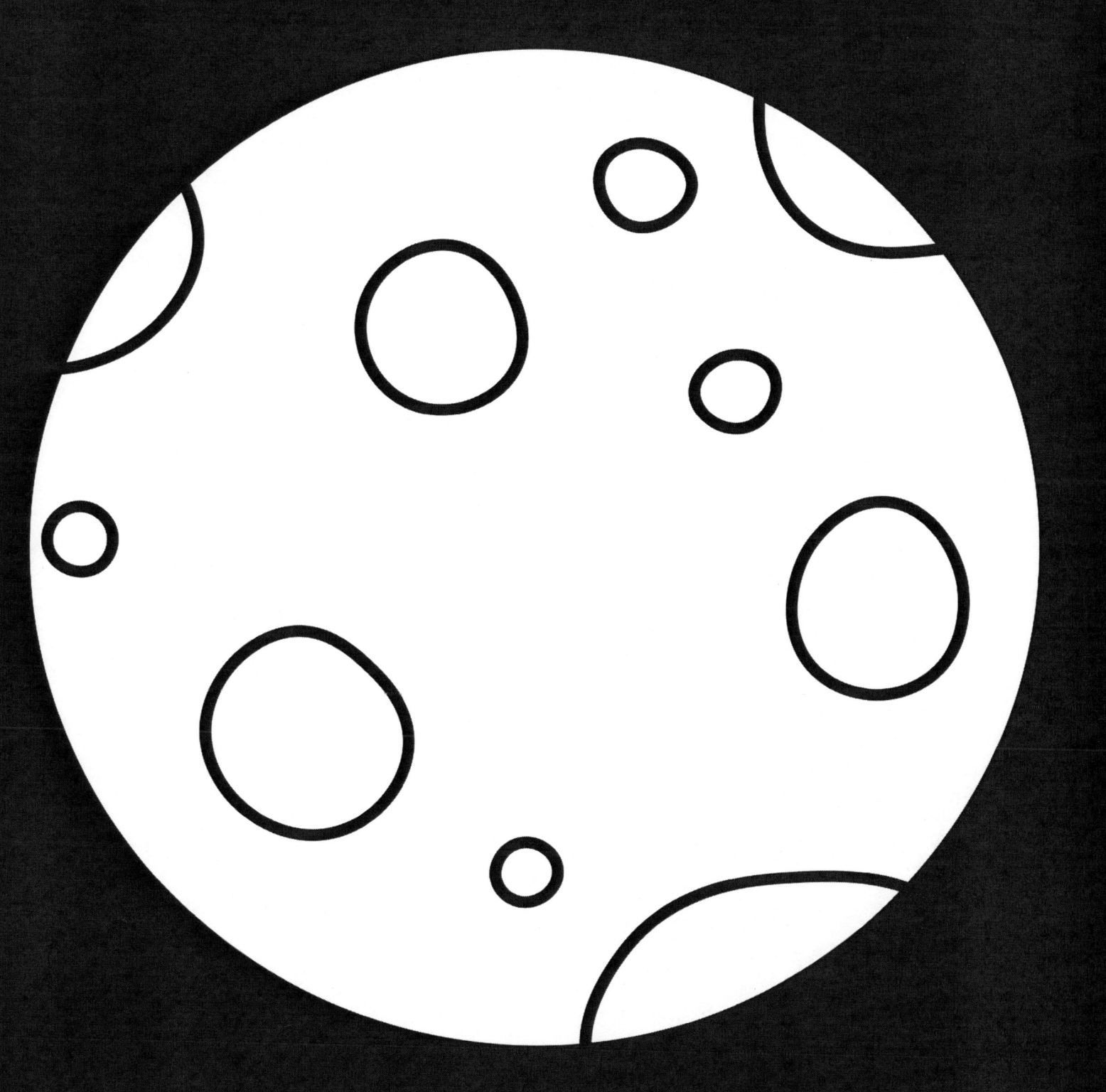

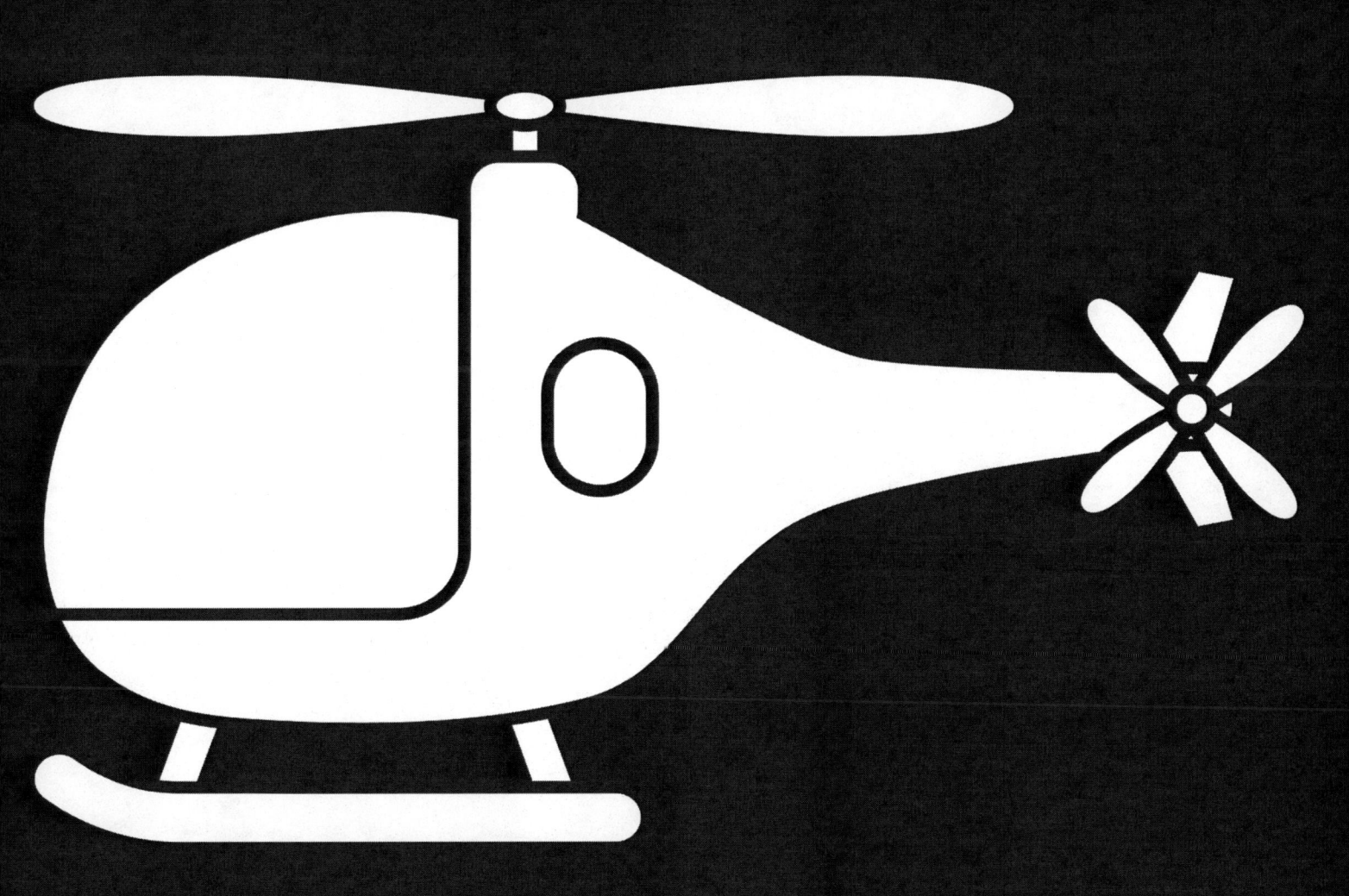

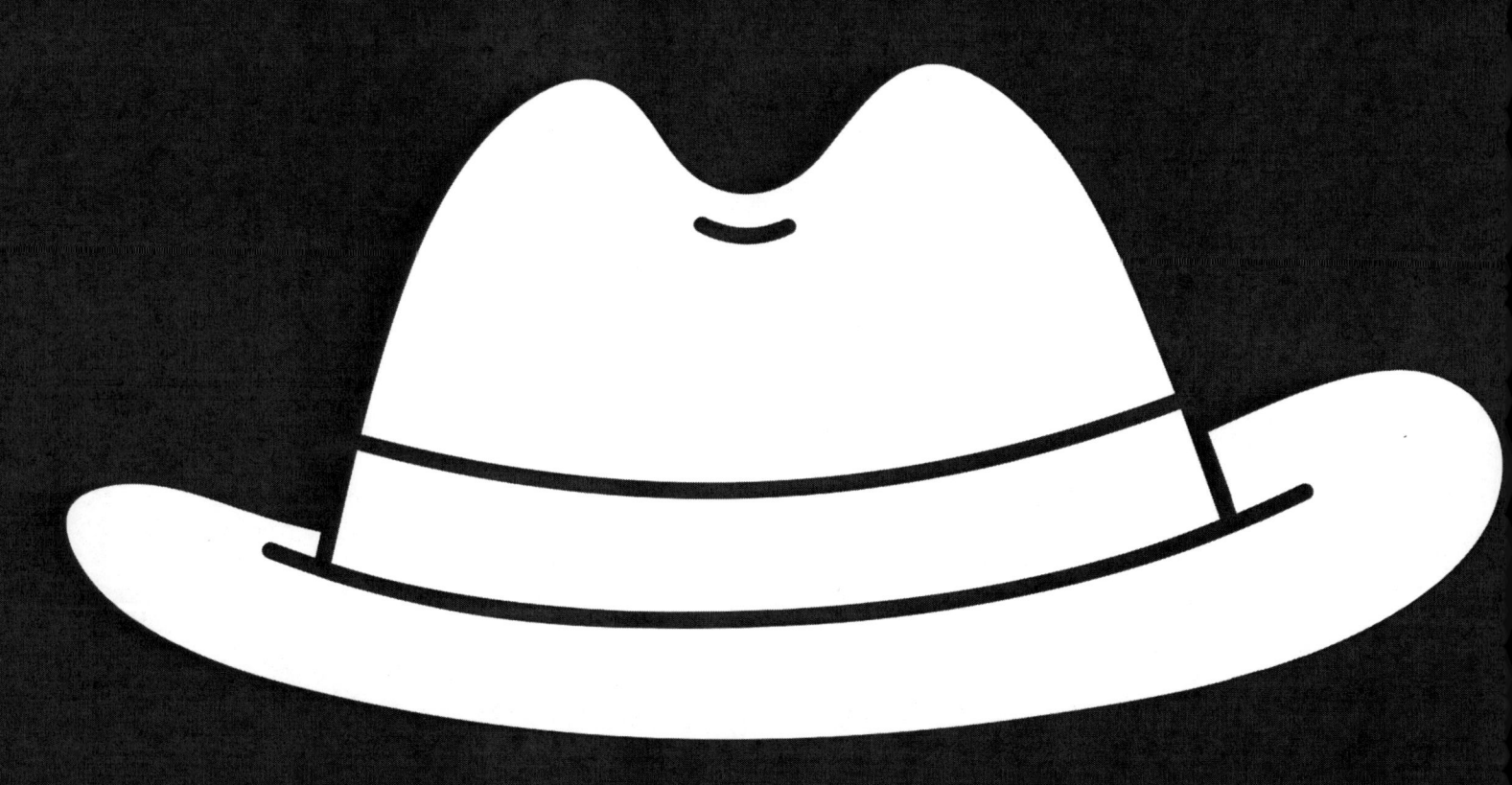

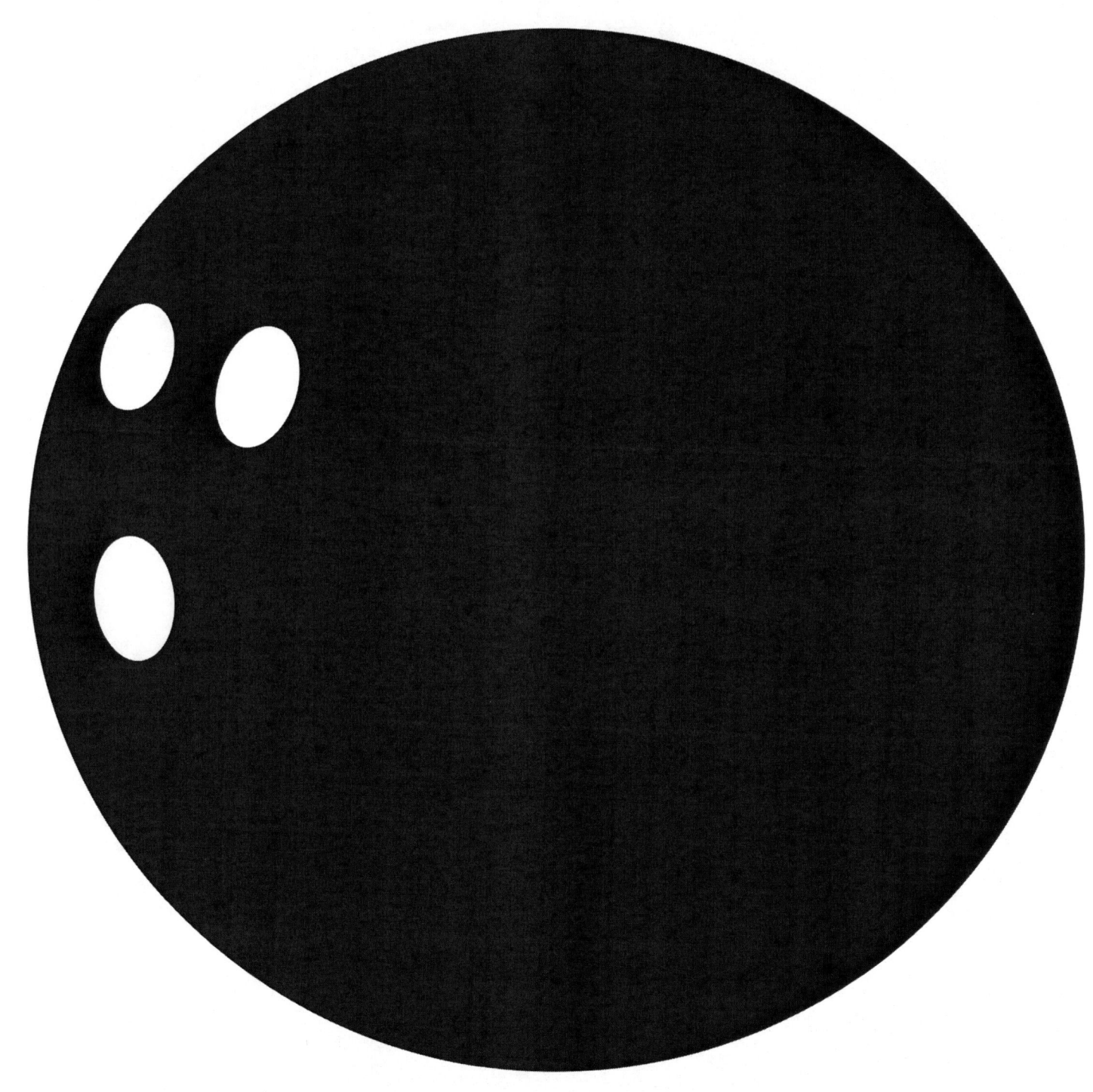

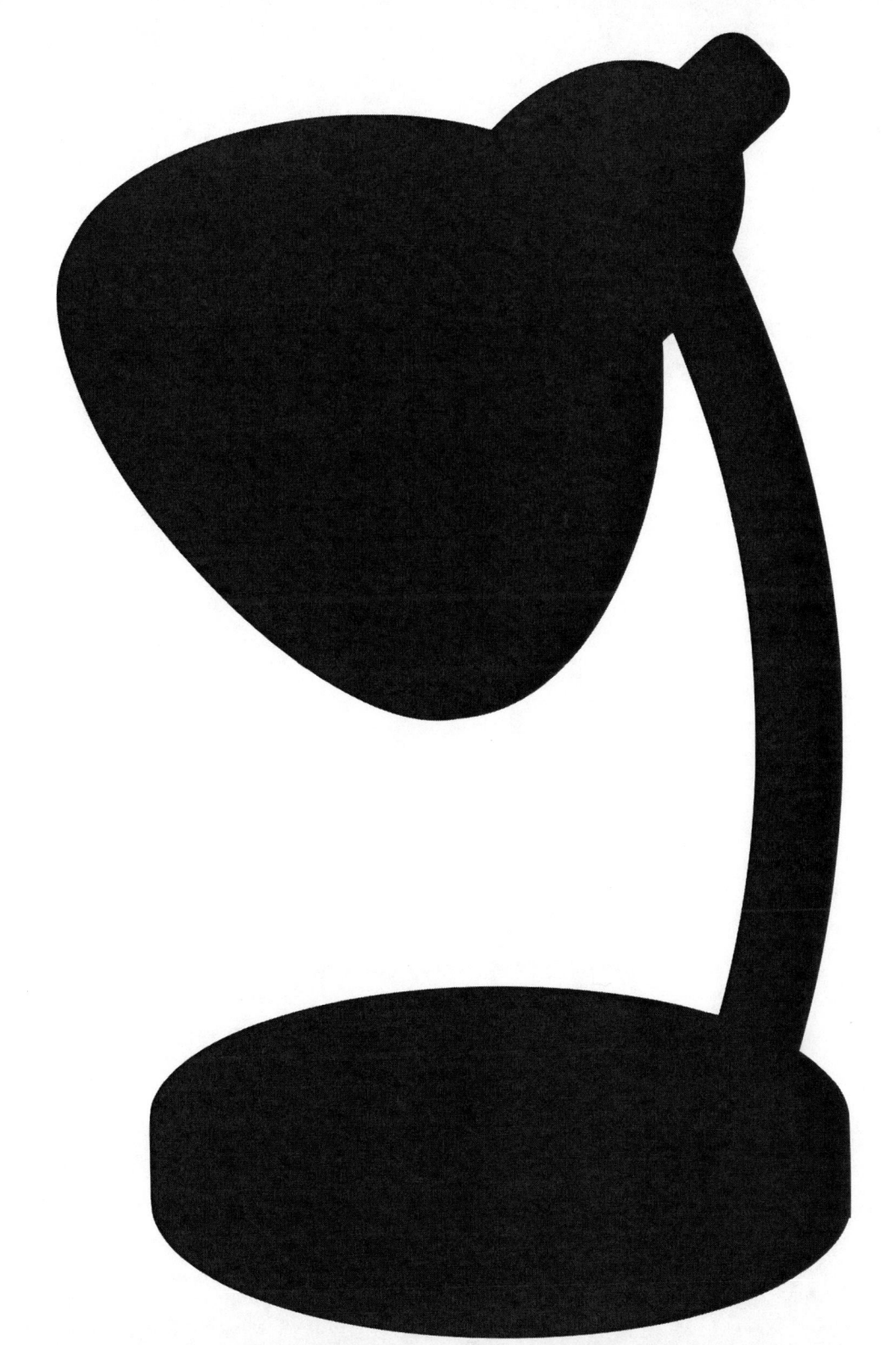

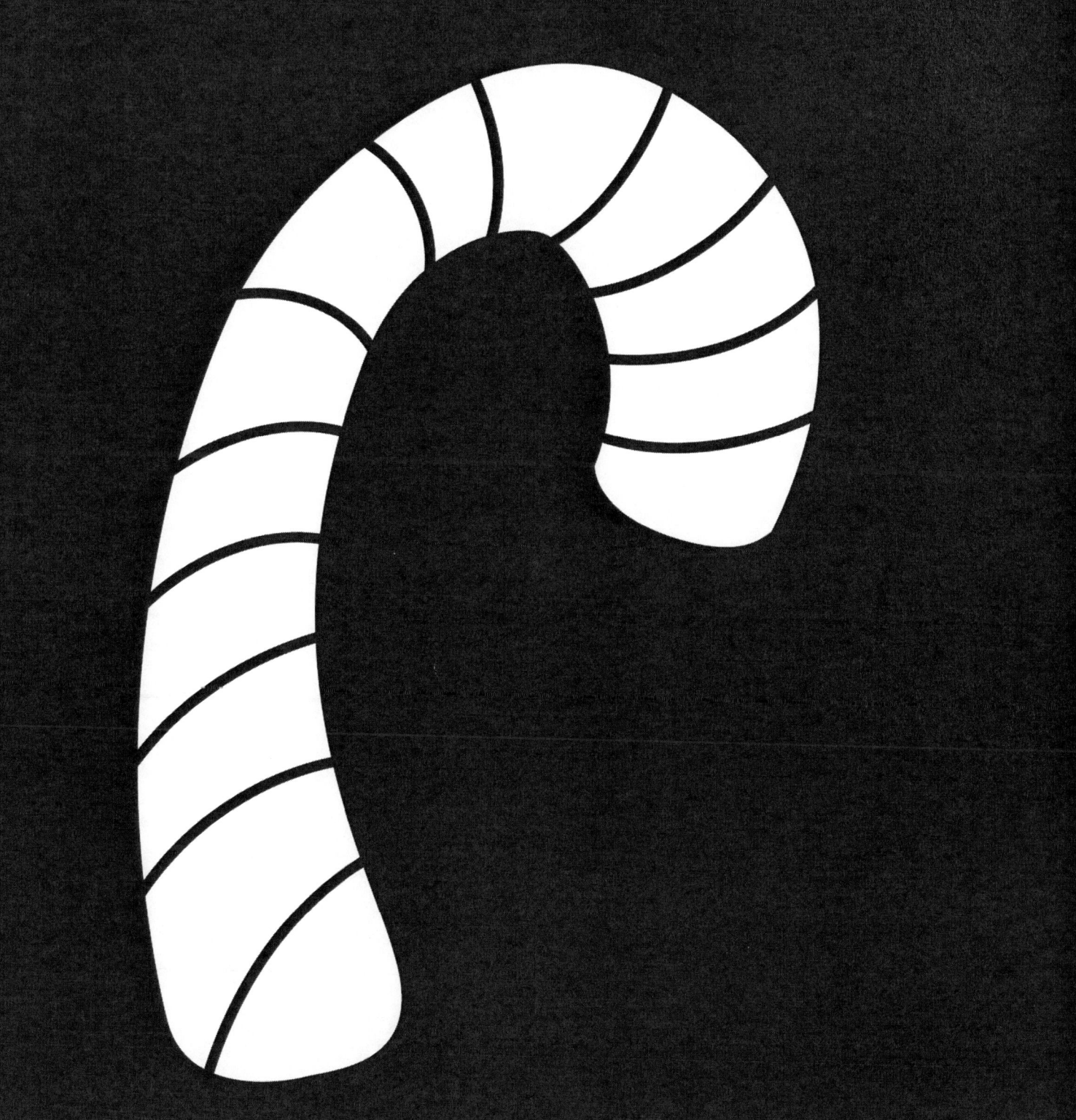

Thank you!

Thank you for purchase!

If you enjoyed this book, please consider leaving us a review! It takes few seconds, but your feedback is essential in helping us improve and craft future book that engage, entertain, and educate young minds like yours!

Manufactured by Amazon.ca
Acheson, AB